Celebration
Dramas for Christmas

**Alice Bass, Lisa Gaylord, Doug Kotwica,
Stephen W. Pavey, Tim Wesemann, Marshal Younger**

SAINT LOUIS

Copyright © 1999 Concordia Publishing House
3558 S. Jefferson Avenue, St. Louis, MO 63118-3968
Manufactured in the United States of America

Library of Congress Cataloging-in-Publication Data

Celebration : dramas for Christmas / Alice Bass ... [et al.].
    p.   cm. — (Intermission scripts)
  Includes index.
  ISBN 0-570-05387-0
  1. Christmas plays, American. I. Series. II. Bass, Alice.
PS627.C57 C4   1999
246'.72 21—dc21   99-044223

1   2   3   4   5   6   7   8   9   10   08   07   06   05   04   03   02   01   00   99

Contents

Introduction

Thanks be to God for His indescribable gift! 2 Corinthians 9:15

The image is a familiar one, sung about in songs and adorning Christmas cards world-wide: a small stable or cave-like setting, with mother and father peering joyfully down at a smiling, peaceful, transcendent child. A golden light touches everything—including cows and sheep—and for one brief, captured moment, all is right with the world.

Another image is perhaps just as familiar: a dark hillside, scraggly sheep guarded by scraggly shepherds, all kneeling while the heavens fill with bright lights and angelic faces. The initial terror of the shepherds, brought on by the appearance of one angel, not to mention a heavenly host, is never shown; merely more peace and tranquility. Once again, the image says, all is right with the world.

Is it?

Modern-day celebrations of Christmas leave little room for picture-perfect ideals. If we manage to spare a moment from shopping and family gatherings, we may sing about a baby born in Bethlehem, and shepherds guarding their flocks. We may take one quiet moment in a candle-illuminated church to reflect on the silence and holiness of a night long ago. We may lift wondering eyes to a clear, star-sprinkled sky and have a brief understanding of the word *peace.*

But is all really right with the world—with ourselves?

In a less-than-idyllic setting, a Child was born into the world. Others were probably born that night; many others have been born since. But with the birth of this particular Child, the darkness and depravity and sin of the world were illuminated by the light of God's love. This birth was a moment of eternal hope, of eternal salvation. This birth was a moment where the fear of the shepherds—the fear living in us all—was drowned out by the glorious celebration of a host of angels.

Today, when war, disease, hatred, bitterness, and darkness seem to have overtaken our world and our souls, we may be hard-pressed to see the light or hear the song of the angels. We may be content and may, in some cases, have no other choice but to leave idyllic Christmas-card images on Christmas cards, and leave that moment of peace for a brief glance at the sky. But God's arrival into the world through the birth of His Son is not just a momentary, passing, fleeting glance into hope and salvation. Instead, it is an eternal celebration of the triumph of love and grace; a celebration held world-wide in the hearts and lives of all humanity.

This Christmas, shop for presents and spend time with family. But most important, stand apart from darkness and mayhem and in quietness, in joyfulness, in peacefulness, in holiness, join the celebration of angels and humanity: for unto us, this day, was born God's indescribable Gift. And all is, indeed, right with the world.

Production Notes
Using Drama

How do you use drama in worship? How will the congregation react? What is an appropriate response to drama in church? Who will direct? Who will act? What is the pastor's involvement? If you're just starting to use drama in your worship services and Sunday school or Bible study classes, you're probably asking some of these questions. We'd like to help you find the answers.

Drama and the Church

Drama has been a part of the church since Jesus' time. Take a look at the parables. Through them we see that Jesus wasn't a talking head. He realized people would better understand and retain what He told them if He spoke in word pictures. Drama is a natural extension of such word pictures. "Religious" drama re-creates and re-presents the amazing acts of God and His intercessions in human life. What better way to understand the passion of our Lord than through drama? What better way to understand our relationships with one another and with our Lord than through drama? Drama isn't "religious" merely because of its subject matter. Drama is religious when it arouses the audience's attention so they walk away with renewed spirits, exalted hearts, and a clearer understanding of God's work in their lives. Drama is religious when it forces us to confront our beliefs on the deepest spiritual level and, in that con-frontation, to more clearly see ourselves in relation to our God.

That said, you have an awesome task. You have the privilege of using a tool that reaches and teaches the masses. You have the responsibility of making drama "religious."

So What Is Drama?

Drama for use in the church needs to meet the same criteria as drama for use in a theater:

1. It must have a point and make it.

2. The characters need to be realistic and believable (even in a farce, comedy, or reader's theater). They must be well-developed and convey realistic emotion.

3. The drama must have conflict. That doesn't mean that characters have to argue or fight; it means there must be a struggle between opposing forces—internal or external.

4. The drama must have a clear arc from beginning to middle to end. It must also have a clear climax. If the drama is to stand alone, it should have a clear resolution. There is a difference between resolution and conclusion. A resolution resolves the conflict; a conclusion brings a closing to the situation. If the drama is to be used as a sermon starter, it does not require a clear resolution of the conflict. The

pastor will use the drama as a jumping-off point for his sermon; he will bring resolution to the conflict.

It's important that the drama have a point so it doesn't become mere entertainment during the worship service or Bible study. Drama, used correctly, can be an effective teaching tool. Used incorrectly it becomes a distraction.

Tips for Producing Drama

Most of the dramas in this book are brief enough to be used as *part* of a worship, devotional, or classroom setting. (Some are longer and can be used as a complete presentation.) Short dramas allow for minimal rehearsal and easy line memorization. Here are a few tips as you work with drama in your church.

1. *Let the drama serve the Word.* In most cases, especially when presented as part of a worship service, drama assists and enhances the reading and preaching of the Word. Each script in this collection includes at least one Scripture reference as well as questions for study and discussion and notes for the pastor or Bible study leader. Dramas used to set up a sermon sometimes leave the audience begging for the Gospel message. At other times, the drama raises a question or evokes emotion or thought on a particular subject. In each instance, drama is an effective tool for teaching the Word of God: A pastor may choose to use a drama before, during, or after his sermon. A teacher may use drama to get students ready for the lesson. Or a drama can be used as a chil-

dren's message, offering children a new way of understanding and responding to the Gospel. However it is used, it should enhance, not replace, the teaching of the Word.

2. *Recruit your actors.* Your actors should know something of the craft of acting. It may be difficult, but avoid asking for volunteers to serve as actors. Recruit people with a gift for and some experience in acting. That's not to say you can never use a novice. Sometimes they surprise you and, with a little extra coaching, can be effective members of the drama ministry. But most often, a team of volunteer actors who have never had any stage experience outside the annual Christmas pageant, doesn't make for an effective drama ministry. Compare your drama team to a church choir. Many church choirs are well-organized and have committed members who know something about music. So it should be with your drama ministry. Acting is a skill as is singing. The choir director doesn't allow just anyone to sing a solo—you should be as careful in selecting your actors. Likewise, the choir director is probably a trained musician. The drama director should be trained in his or her craft as well. Find someone in your congregation who has some professional theater experience or who has studied theater. His or her experience and training will add to the professionalism of your performances.

3. *Rehearse.* Though many of the dramas here are brief, they still need

rehearsal time. You can't hand out scripts on Saturday afternoon and expect a stellar performance on Sunday morning. Get scripts to the actors early enough so they have time to memorize their lines. Walk through the drama several times with scripts in hand, then come back and rehearse again after lines are memorized. Take time before rehearsal to go through the script yourself. Figure out what it is saying and decide how best to share that message with your audience. Use the purpose statement and theme for the script to guide your reflections. Go into the first rehearsal prepared with blocking ideas, a clear understanding of the subtext, and a knowledge of the script's arc from beginning to middle to end. The more prepared you are before the first rehearsal, the better the rehearsal and performance. Remember to be flexible. If an actor has another idea for blocking or is reading subtext differently than you are, talk about it and come to an agreement.

4. *Strive for more than bathrobes and sandals.* The church expects excellence from its musicians and preachers; it should expect no less from its drama performances. Many of the dramas need little or no set but where a set is required, it should enhance the drama. Be realistic with costuming. Don't use bathrobes and sandals for biblical costumes. Plan ahead enough to have a committee of people (who know something about sewing and costuming) design and build realistic costumes. Work with the actors to develop characters and to understand the subtext in the script. If at all possible, use professional theatrical lighting. It can enhance a script tremendously. We understand that you may not have these things available, so the scripts work just fine without them. Throughout this book, theatrical terminology such as center stage, down left, stage right, etc. was used for consistency. If you are unfamiliar with these terms, have no fear—simply use the stage layout on page 11 to help you. (Note: UR is upstage right, or, simply, up right. URC is up right center, and so on. All stage directions are from the actor's point of view as he faces the audience.) And remember that these dramas can be performed in a variety of settings: a classroom, the chancel, a multi-purpose room, etc. Adapt the stage directions to work in your own space.

5. *Work with the pastor.* Ask your pastor how he wants to incorporate the drama. Does he want to look at a drama you chose first and have one theme throughout the service, supported by the drama, his sermon, and the music? Does he want to give you a service theme and ask you to find a drama to match it? Does he want to look at a script first and write his sermon to go with it? These are all good options. Good communication with your pastor helps to incorporate drama as part of the worship experience.

So you're ready to get started. Whether you're just getting your feet wet with using drama in your church or you're ready to start a full-fledged drama ministry, it is our prayer that these dramas are useful tools as you spread God's mighty Word.

The Editors

UPSTAGE

UR	URC	UC	ULC	UL
R	RC	C	LC	L
DR	DRC	DC	DLC	DL

STAGE RIGHT

STAGE LEFT

DOWNSTAGE

AUDIENCE

Production Notes
Using Monologues

Monologues are an effective dramatic tool because they allow the audience to peer into the heart and mind of a single character. That's also what makes them difficult to perform well. In a sketch or other script with multiple actors, the cast is working together toward the common goal of getting the message out. With a monologue, that responsibility falls on one person's shoulders.

For a monologue to work well, it must be rehearsed. The performance should seem like a natural flow of thought and emotion from the character, not a recitation. To help the actor prepare for the performance, break the monologue into beats—sections which contain a single thought. Have the actor write out the character's motivation for each beat as well as for the monologue overall. Rehearse with script in hand before the actor memorizes so he or she can internalize the motivations and subtext. Next, work with the actor to discover blocking. What motivates this character's movements? Where is the character? Is he or she alone or is the monologue delivered like a secret whispered to a friend? Help the actor answer these questions as you work with him or her through the rehearsal process. The result will be a poignant moment between the character and the audience.

A Moment Longed for

by Alice Bass

Purpose: To explore the reality of Mary's experience as a new mother

Theme: Christmas; Mary's perspective on Jesus' birth

Scripture: Luke 2:16–19

Time: 2–3 minutes

Cast: **Mary**—young mother of Jesus

Costumes: Floor-length tunic and shawl for her head

Props: None

Lighting: General

Sound: No sound effects necessary

Setting: First-century Bethlehem

A Moment Longed for

by Alice Bass

MARY

I haven't yet had a chance to take a good, deep, clean, breath of air. The whole trip here I kept thinking—if only I could get inside, take a cool breath, and shake this dust out of my lungs. But once inside this cave, well ... the air was so heavy and humid from all the animals. Each pain seemed heavier as I felt the weight of their breath pressing down on me. Joseph picked up the pattern of my strained breaths in an effort to help me. But I began to feel more and more stifled.

Then suddenly, He was here. He was in our arms. All breathing stopped. I slowly took in the sweetness of Him. And I was lost. My thoughts swirled around me as if I was in a windstorm. I couldn't remember how we came to be here. I wanted to remember all You had said about the Baby. Images of You, Father, nourishing me, lifting me up, giving me strength, went through me as I held and nourished Him. I looked at His fingers and could not understand how You could be in these tiny hands. I wanted to cry out to Joseph, "Tell me everything the angel said to you! To me!"

Instead, I held my breath, straining to hear His dropping in and out. As I laid Him down, it seemed I would finally get my moment to ask You all the questions in my heart, finally a moment to breathe and quietly listen to You. But then the stable was filled with shepherds; surrounding me, peering over me trying to see the Baby. I felt like grabbing Him and hiding Him from them. I wanted to keep Him for myself.

Then I heard sighs from those rough men. Looking at their faces ... humble, soft, mouths open, some weeping. Hearing their story, how they came to be here ... the sounds of the animals, the damp air, the crunching of the straw ... It is a symphony! A song of joy to You, for what You have done. My breath is no longer stifled but I feel as if my lungs will burst with air! I wonder no more, but take it all in, draw all these things into my heart to ponder, to savor. *(MARY draws a deep breath in and lets it out slowly, smiling.)*

Lights fade to blackout.

A Moment Longed for

by Alice Bass

A Note to the Pastor or Bible Study Leader:

"But Mary treasured all these things and pondered them in her heart" (Luke 2:19).

Of all the characters in the Christmas drama (excepting Jesus, of course) Mary ironically emerges as the most vulnerable yet most powerful. She claims the center spotlight in most Christmas pageants, as well she should; a frail teenager cradling a small bundle of blankets or a plastic doll in her arms, looking properly bewildered. Often, at times, a bit too peaceful. Who can imagine what it must have been like for her to be so far from home, from her community of support, in a town of strangers, giving birth in a barn? Her only sustenance, outside of gentle Joseph, was her faith.

It was this faith of Mary's that inspired Martin Luther to write: "had she not believed she could not have conceived." For the great Reformer, Mary was the paragon of faith—having the capacity to hear the promise of an angel and then to risk all to follow. In so doing she follows in the footsteps of Sarah, mother of the Covenant. Unlike Sarah, however, Mary finds the promise of the angel no laughing matter (Genesis 18). A soft "let it be to me according to Your word" sets her off on a journey to Bethlehem and admiration.

The "cults of Mary" that have emerged throughout history switch the spotlight from the faith to the woman, dangerously deifying this simple servant of God. Such excesses need not deter the faithful pastor, however, from "pondering" alongside her in this Christmas season. The word "ponder" carries a root meaning of "to weigh," and there is so much to weigh as Christmas dawns upon us. That the almighty God would take flesh within the womb of this child raises the question of how God might wish to take flesh within all of His faithful servants. Let's take time to ponder with Mary this year!

Questions for Study and Discussion:

1. What might Mary teach us about discipleship in today's culture? What lessons do you need to learn?

2. How does God wish to take flesh within you this Christmas? How do you witness to God's becoming flesh in Jesus?

3. If you could ask Mary any one question about her Advent-Christmas adventure, what would it be?

A Father's Role

by Alice Bass

Purpose: To explore Joseph's important role in the Christmas story

Theme: Christmas; Joseph's perspective on the incarnation

Scripture: Matthew 1:18–2:15

Time: 2–3 minutes

Cast: **Joseph**—age 25–35

Costumes: Floor-length tunic, sandals, head covering

Props: Staff

Lighting: General

Sound: No sound effects necessary

Setting: First-century Bethlehem; manger scene or bare stage

Notes: This monologue may be performed immediately following *A Moment Longed for,* which is from Mary's perspective, or they may be performed on different Sundays during the Christmas season. A key for the actor here is not to focus on the historical character of Joseph but to create a new father who is experiencing fear. Joseph is beginning to understand that he plays an important role in this unique family.

A Father's Role

by Alice Bass

JOSEPH

They sleep so peacefully. It's hard to imagine that they're anything but ordinary ... His mother had so much trouble having Him. I can still feel her fear ... and the pain. I remember thinking, let me have the burden of her pain. She's been through so much already ...

And He wasn't born under the greatest of conditions. I mean, I tried, I really did try, but the place was so full and it was time and ... and then it was too late. The sound, the smells, the cries all seemed to hit me at once. And then ... there He was. Tiny and red and wrinkled and ... beautiful. And suddenly nothing and everything seemed important at the same time. The months before were a blur. And I kept thinking ... this is our child. He will look up to me. He will question me. He will learn from me ... and I from Him. I've heard people, even my own family, speak of miracles. *This* is a miracle. My son.

But He's more than my son. A host of heaven appeared to shepherds and they came to worship Him. I want to bow before Him too. How can I raise a child I'm in awe of? What can I possibly say or do for Him?

And His mother—what kind of husband can I be to her? God chose her to carry the King! I've always wanted to be a leader for my wife and children. A man of confidence and quietness. The kind of father who inspires obedience and greatness. How can I do that now? Next to Him I'm insignificant, small, unable to *do* anything, much less lead this family.

JOSEPH kneels and looks at the manger. He is struck with a thought.

But the Father said, "Joseph, son of David ... do not be afraid to take Mary home as your wife ..." *Do not be afraid.* That's what the angels told the shepherds too. *Do not be afraid.*

JOSEPH is quiet and contemplative for a moment, still looking at the manger.

Amazing. They seem so delicate. Who could know they're anything but ordinary ...

Lights fade out.

A Father's Role

by Alice Bass

A Note to the Pastor or Bible Study Leader:

How wonderful it would be to have more information on Joseph. It is strange that we do not. Mattew traces his genealogy (Matthew 1:1–16) in order to verify that Jesus was a true son of David and Abraham. We are told that he was a craftsman from Nazareth. His age is not known, although it is assumed that he was considerably older than Mary. The last we see of him in the Gospels is at Jesus' adventure as a 12-year-old in the Jerusalem temple (Luke 2:41–51).

Matthew presents Joseph as a "righteous man," a true Jew who nonetheless was willing to side-step the law when he discovered Mary's pregnancy. He would "divorce her quietly" rather than shame her (Matthew 1:19). Here too is a man of compassion. But above righteousness and compassion, Matthew emphasizes Joseph's faith. Like his beloved spouse, Joseph sets aside reasonableness to follow the commands of God through the angels. It happens to him, as to his Patriarch Joseph, in dreams. Joseph hears the words of the angels, and obeys.

In the drama, Joseph struggles with his role as father and husband, having been cast into a most unusual (to say the least!) situation. Men who marry and parent in our 21st century culture share similar struggles as shifting roles within the home, family structure, and market-place seem to make obsolete the traditional role of father as "head of the house," and "breadwinner."

What might Joseph teach us?

Openness to God's speaking, and faithfulness to God's commands are high on the list! Joseph teaches us the virtue of acting boldly when confronted with the conflicting demands of the culture and conscience (the law says "put away" Mary), as well as confrontation with evil (Herod). Though Joseph is a strong "bit player" in the Christmas drama, he nonetheless is absolutely necessary. Though we know very little about him historically, his strong witness infuses the Christmas Gospel with strength and faith!

Questions for Study and Discussion:

1. How do you react to the drama's depiction of Joseph? What additional words would you put into his mouth? What might you omit?

2. When Matthew describes the coming of the Wise Men (Matthew 1:11) he tells us that when they entered the house they saw "the child with His mother Mary." Why do you think Matthew omits Joseph?

3. If you were to ask Joseph any question about his role in the Christmas story, what would it be? How do you think he might answer?

4. How does it feel to you to be a "bit player" in life's dramas? How can God use your contribution, often insignificant, to accomplish His will?

Production Notes
Using Sketches

Sketches are perhaps the easiest form of drama to use in worship. They are often light-hearted and short which makes them fun to work on. They are frequently used to set up a sermon so they don't have to resolve any conflict. And they usually don't have any Gospel message on their own—it's supplied by the pastor in his message following the drama. But they require rehearsal all the same. Because sketches are short, there is less time to make the point. Actors need to be sharp and well rehearsed.

You'll find that most of our sketches have small casts and require little or no set. The focus is not on the theatrics but on getting the message across. Let that be your focus as well as you prepare for performance. Work with the actors on blocking, characterization, line memorization, and timing. Discuss the message of the script with the cast so you're all telling the same story. Work with the pastor to determine what part the sketch plays in the service and how he plans to resolve the conflict or situation set up in the script.

Keep the performance simple so the message is clear.

The Joseph Show

by Marshal Younger

Purpose: To explore our role as members of Christ's body, the Church; to explore our need for significance

Theme: Evangelism; witnessing; body of Christ; Christmas

Scripture: Ephesians 4:1–7, 11–16

Time: 2–3 minutes

Cast: **Mark**—the director of the Christmas play

Narrator—(in the Christmas play)

Shepherd 1—(in the Christmas play)

Shepherd 2—(in the Christmas play)

Sheep 1—(in the Christmas play)

Angel—(in the Christmas play)

Lee—a teenager working in the church

Steve—a voice over the P.A. system

Costumes: Casual, contemporary dress; set during an early rehearsal so no "Christmas play costumes" are necessary

Props: Scripts for all characters but Lee and Steve, piece of paper for Lee

Lighting: General

Sound: Sound effect tape of torrential downpour

Setting: A church, in the middle of a rehearsal for the Christmas play

Notes: Because this sketch takes place during a rehearsal, most actors can carry their scripts. They may read any lines that are part of the Christmas play they are rehearsing, but all other dialogue should be memorized.

The Joseph Show

by Marshal Younger

The middle of a rehearsal for a Christmas play. The SHEPHERDS are keeping watch over their flocks by night. SHEEP 1 is on all fours, acting like a SHEEP. NARRATOR, fully downstage and off to the side, begins reading off a script.

NARRATOR

And in the same region there were some shepherds staying out in the fields, keeping watch over their flocks by night.

SHEPHERD 1

It's cold out tonight.

SHEPHERD 2

Very. Cold and lonely. Kind of like ... my heart.

SHEPHERD 1

(Confused) What?

SHEPHERD 2

I have something to tell you, Marco. I've been transferred.

SHEPHERD 1

(Looking out toward audience, confused) What are you talking about?

SHEPHERD 2

They've got me taking a flock up near Mount Horeb. My wife is upset. We have to leave her family now. Plus, we have friends here; we really wanted to grow some roots ... *(Beginning to cry)* My life is always so random. *(Shouting to the sky, dramatically)* Why?!

DIRECTOR rises from the audience and crosses toward the actors.

DIRECTOR

Stop! Stop! *(EVERYONE on stage is disgusted.)* Joe, what are you doing?

SHEPHERD 2

Acting.

DIRECTOR

None of that is in the script! You're supposed to say, "Yes, it's cold. And lonely." And then the angel comes out. That's it. What was all that?

SHEPHERD 2

A little ad-lib.

DIRECTOR

A little one?

SHEPHERD 2

I'm just trying to give the shepherd some character, you know. He's so one-dimensional.

DIRECTOR

It doesn't matter. This play is not about you.

SHEPHERD 1

(To the DIRECTOR) Hey, is my name really Marco?

DIRECTOR

No.

SHEPHERD 2

Then what should I call him?

DIRECTOR

Nothing. You never use his name.

SHEPHERD 2

You see, that's what I'm talking about. These shepherds don't even have names. It's like they don't even matter. Joseph has a name. Mary has a name.

DIRECTOR

That's because they're main characters.

SHEPHERD 2

So why can't I be a main character?

DIRECTOR

Because you're a shepherd.

SHEPHERD 2

Being a shepherd is boring. I wanna be Joseph.

DIRECTOR

We already have a Joseph.

SHEPHERD 2

Shepherd number two has virtually no impact on this play. I want to make a difference. Like Joseph.

DIRECTOR

You can make a difference by being Shepherd number two. That's if you play it correctly. Now let's try it again. Places, everyone. And play it straight this time, okay? *(Beat)* And does anyone know why it's so cold in here?

No answer. EVERYONE takes their positions, SHEPHERD 2 with a scowl.

DIRECTOR

Okay, let's take it from the narrator.

NARRATOR

And in the same region there were some shepherds staying out in the fields, keeping watch over their flocks by night.

SHEPHERD 1

It's cold out tonight.

SHEPHERD 2

Very. Cold and lonely.

ANGEL ENTERS. The SHEPHERDS are scared. SHEEP 1 runs over to the ANGEL and begins to rub against her leg. ANGEL is thrown off by this.

ANGEL

Do not be afraid. For ... *(Distracted by SHEEP 1)* For I bring you ... *(To DIRECTOR)* What is this sheep doing?

DIRECTOR

Stop! Hang on! *(To SHEEP 1)* Jeremy, what's going on?

SHEEP 1

What?

DIRECTOR

Why are you touching the angel?

SHEEP

It was just an idea I had.

DIRECTOR

Uh huh.

SHEEP 1

Just listen. You know how they say that animals can sense if someone's nice? I think it would be really symbolic of man's misunderstanding of the supernatural if the sheep knows the truth about angels even more than people do. If the shepherds are more afraid than the sheep, I think it says a lot about man's relationship with forces beyond—

DIRECTOR

What does that have to do with the play?

SHEEP 1

In essence, everything!

DIRECTOR

You're a sheep!

SHEEP 1

Exactly!

DIRECTOR

Your job is to walk around and make sheep noises, not a philosophical statement.

SHEEP 1

Make sheep noises? I think I have more to contribute to this play than that.

DIRECTOR

No, you don't.

SHEEP 1

Maybe I can try to comfort the shepherds by putting my paw up on their arms ...

DIRECTOR

Don't touch the shepherds.

SHEEP 1

If I was Joseph you'd let me touch the shepherds.

DIRECTOR

You're not Joseph.

SHEEP 1

I wanna be Joseph. I want a big part. This little sheep part is having no creative impact on this play.

DIRECTOR

That's okay. You don't have to. But somebody has to play the sheep!

SHEEP 1

But ... this part is not satisfying my creative hungers.

DIRECTOR

Eat a Snickers bar! Everyone in their places! *(Beat)* Is it just me or is it really cold in here?

EVERYONE begins to go back to their places. LEE ENTERS. He is holding a piece of paper.

LEE

Hey, I think I know why it's so cold.

DIRECTOR

Why?

LEE

This note was attached to the thermostat. It's from Pete the janitor.

DIRECTOR

Read it.

LEE

Dear Church, I'm tired of being the insignificant little janitor. I feel like I'm having no effect on this church or the community around it. So I quit. I'm going to seminary to become a televangelist. Signed, Pete.

DIRECTOR

Oh, great! Lee, see if you can fix the thermostat. *(LEE EXITS.)* I guess we have to practice in the cold for awhile, people. Places. Let's start with the narrator.

NARRATOR

And in the same region there were some shepherds staying out in the fields, keeping watch over their flocks by night.

DIRECTOR

(To someone behind him) Okay, can we get some outdoor sound effects and sheep grazing?

Suddenly we hear the sounds of a torrential downpour.

DIRECTOR

Wait! Hold it! We don't want a storm!

STEVE

(Unseen, over the P.A. system) I was just trying to give the scene a feeling of restlessness.

DIRECTOR

I want sheep! That's it!

STEVE

It's just that I don't feel like I'm contributing to the play very much.

DIRECTOR

You don't have to. Don't you people see? Somebody has to do the little stuff. The small parts are just as important as the big ones. Without someone to play the small parts, this play doesn't happen!

STEVE

(Muttering) If I was Joseph, you'd let me make whatever sound effects I wanted.

DIRECTOR

You know what? I can't take this anymore. I've gotta get outta here. *(DIRECTOR EXITS.)*

ACTORS look around at one another for a moment.

SHEEP 1

Cool. I wanted to direct anyway. Places, everyone!

SHEPHERD 2

Wait. I want to direct!

ANGEL

I'd do a better job than either of you two ...

As they ad-lib their desires to be the director, they push each other offstage and EXIT.

The Joseph Show

by Marshal Younger

A Note to the Pastor or Bible Study Leader:

At Christmas we are all "bit" players, the show's "extras" who defer in wonder to the King of Kings. The culture prizes self-expression and self-realization, but Christians see that when God wants to express Himself to the world, He did so as an infant in a barn, the paradigm of humility. Peruse Christmas advertising today and you'll find plenty of sermonic illustration for the contrast between the humility of the Christ Child and the self-absorption of the age.

In this drama, the director is only half right when he tells the shepherd, "this play is not about you." In fact, the drama of Christmas is lovingly about all of us; about each individual and her or his salvation. St. Augustine wrote: "He loves each of us as though there were only one of us." It is, ironically, as we put aside our need for self-gratification that we receive the greatest affirmation of self at Christmas!

Questions for Study and Discussion:

1. How does our culture promote an ego-centered celebration of the Savior's birth? (Note: search and display Christmas ads from magazines and newpapers.)

2. Worship calls us to abandon self in an outpouring of adoration to God. How does that happen in your congragation's worship? In your own individual worship?

3. The director in the script said, "Without someone to play the small parts, this play doesn't happen." What small parts are happening in your congregation over this Christmas celebration? In worship? In children's ministry? In social outreach? Who is playing these roles? (Include a prayer thanking God for the small roles and the "bit players" in your congregation who make the drama of Christmas come alive.)

The New Christmas Story

by Lisa Gaylord

Purpose:	To reveal the simplicity of the Christmas story
Theme:	Christmas; salvation
Scripture:	John 3:16; Luke 2
Time:	5–7 minutes
Cast:	**Sally**—flighty and friendly
	Denise—serious and cautious
Costumes:	"Sunday best" for Denise; casual dress for Sally
Props:	None
Lighting:	General
Sound:	No sound effects necessary
Setting:	A church sanctuary or Sunday school room

The New Christmas Story

by Lisa Gaylord

DENISE

Hi, kids. We have a special treat tonight. Sally is here because she wants to share the Christmas story with all of you! *(DENISE begins to move off but comes back quickly when SALLY finishes her first lines.)*

SALLY

That's right! I'm really excited about it because I'm going to tell you a Christmas story no one has ever heard before.

DENISE

Excuse me, did you say a Christmas story no one has ever heard before?

SALLY

(Speaks lines without much expression while DENISE nods throughout) That's right. You see, I know that all these kids know all about Mary and how God sent an angel to tell Mary she was going to have a baby and to name Him Jesus and call Him a special name—Immanuel which means God with us. And that eventually Joseph married her and had to go to Bethlehem right when the baby was supposed to be born because the king named Caesar wanted to count everyone in the country so Joseph had to go to Bethlehem, but there was no room in the inn, so Mary ended up having to have the baby in a manger with lots of animals and the angels appeared to the shepherds in the field and they came to see Jesus.

DENISE

That's right. That's the story of Christmas.

SALLY

And the kids all know it?

DENISE

That's right, they probably do. You know the story of Christmas, don't you kids?

KIDS (audience) respond.

SALLY

Well, I know that I was supposed to tell the story of Christmas to this great bunch of kids. So, I thought to myself: do I want to tell the kids a story that they already know? No. I thought I'd maybe make the story just a bit more interesting. So, get cozy, kids, and you can sit down too.

DENISE

Something tells me I'd better stay right here.

SALLY

Suit yourself!

DENISE

I don't know about this, kids!

SALLY

Now, just give me a chance. The kids are gonna love this. Okay, now, once upon a time ...

DENISE

Once upon a time?

SALLY

Shhh! Once upon a time, God said, "The world is ready for a Savior to save them from their sins," so He sent a shiny lamp to Mary. Mary, this really beautiful princess, finds the lamp and rubs it, to sort of clean it up and all of a sudden—poof!—out comes an angel.

DENISE

What!!! Mary was not a princess; she was a Jewish girl in a small town. And the angel was not in a lamp.

SALLY

I know that! I'm just trying to make it more exciting.

DENISE

Exciting! Maybe this isn't such a great idea ...

SALLY

All right! No lamp, no princess, *(To KIDS)* no fun! Now, let's see, where was I? Oh, yes, the angel comes out of the ... the angel suddenly appears and says, "Mary, you're going to have a baby and you will name Him Rumpelstiltskin."

DENISE

No way! Uh uh! The angel said *Immanuel* for an important reason. It means God with us. And that's who Jesus was, He was God and He came to be with us as a human being. Rumpelstiltskin! I can't believe this!

SALLY

Okay, okay, so that one's important. Now, before Mary had the baby and after Joseph had married her, they got some bad news. Caesar, the king, said that everyone had to go to the place where they had been born so they could count everyone. So Joseph put Mary on his motorcycle and they went to Sesame Street.

DENISE

Whoa! Hold it right there!

SALLY

What's the matter now? I put Joseph in the right way and I have Caesar wanting to count everyone.

DENISE

But the motorcycle and Sesame Street?

SALLY

I thought the donkey was kind of dull. You have to admit that a motorcycle is more exciting, right kids? And where else do they count things but on Sesame Street?

DENISE

Well, there were no motorcycles in Israel when Jesus was born and they were counting people in Bethlehem back then, not on Sesame Street! You can't keep telling the kids these silly things.

SALLY

No problem. I'll put back Bethlehem and Eeyore!

DENISE

What was that?

SALLY

The donkey, okay?

DENISE

That's better.

SALLY

Anyway, they go to Bethlehem real late at night, you know. And they try all the hotels: Holiday Inn, Best Western ...

DENISE clears her throat.

SALLY

I mean the Bethlehem Inn. But there's just no room anywhere. Where are they going to go? Who's going to help them? And to make things worse, Mary suddenly realizes that it's time for the baby to be born. So, they call 911 for an ambulance and ...

DENISE

911! There were no phones! They went to the barn of an inn. Jesus was born there and slept in the manger! You're making this all up. You're changing what really happened. And you're giving me a headache!

SALLY

I'm telling an *exciting* story. But, I'll put the barn back and no phone. So, kids, you won't believe what happens next.

DENISE

I'm sure I won't.

SALLY

Well, Mary has her baby and it's a ... girl!

DENISE

Aaaarrrrgggghhhh!!! It can't be a girl, because the Savior God promised is the Son of God and it can't possibly be the Son of God if it wasn't a boy. Mary had a baby boy!

SALLY

Well, don't have a cow! I understand. Maybe I shouldn't have changed the baby to a girl, but I just didn't want the girls to feel bad, you know?

DENISE

(Through clenched teeth) The baby is a boy.

SALLY

Anyway, I'm almost finished now.

DENISE

Finally!

SALLY

So, Mary has a baby boy and they name Him—*(SALLY looks at DENISE)* they name Him Jesus.

DENISE

That's better.

SALLY

Then, this great star appeared over the whole place and guess what happened?

DENISE

I can't even begin to imagine!

SALLY

A great flying saucer appeared out of the star and aliens came out of it and came to see Jesus.

DENISE

No more! I can't stand it! I just can't stand it! Why are you doing all this to the Christmas story?

SALLY

Because I want the kids to enjoy the story. I don't want them to be bored by the same old story they hear all the time.

DENISE

But, don't you see, it's not a story like Cinderella or Peter Pan. Those are stories that you can change around any way you want to because they are just stories. They didn't really happen. But the story of Christmas is about the birth of Jesus and it is history. It really happened! Every part of it is the truth, from the angels to the shepherds. It's all true.

SALLY

I didn't mean to do anything wrong, I just wanted to make it more interesting.

DENISE

What could be more interesting than God's Son coming to earth and being born a baby and angels making visits to Mary and the shepherds? What could be more important than understanding that He came because He loved us enough to live as a person so He could die for our sins and we could be with Him forever in heaven? Maybe the kids have heard about the birth of Jesus before, but we can never tell them a more important, exciting story than the true story of how and why Jesus was born! Okay?

SALLY

Okay, you're right. Sorry, kids. I shouldn't have changed the truth. Jesus' birthday is too important. But I hope this doesn't ruin my chances to come back because I have another story to share with you. It's all about when Noah built the airplane for the animals before it started to snow!

DENISE

(Losing her temper) Out! *(DENISE chases SALLY offstage.)*

The New Christmas Story

by Lisa Gaylord

A Note to the Pastor or Bible Study Leader:

Finding a "new twist" on the Christmas story is the preacher's constant temptation. The very simplicity of Luke's account has invited all manner of cute and novel additions to the editing of his narrative and the creative combining of Luke's account with Matthew's. (Remember the Wise Men? Where are they in Luke?) From talking animals to little drummer boys and even a cranky innkeeper, it would seem Luke and Matthew never do enough to keep us entertained at Christmas.

The story itself, in all its simplicity, touches the heart, but its message is multi-faceted. We come to Christmas each year and hear the old, old story in ever new ways. Children hear of a God who will be ever near to us. Teenagers hear of another teenager (Mary) who is used by God to accomplish a miracle (so how might God use me?). The poor in our midst remember a God who "fills the hungry with good things." The wealthy are warned of impending emptiness apart from this God to whom rich kings offered their wealth.

Though the story remains the same, we come to it with new hungers in the various seasons of our lives. Blessed is the preacher who reads the complexities of the congregation, while delivering the simple, saving, age-old message ever afresh.

Questions for Study and Discussion:

1. What novel re-tellings of the Christmas story have you experienced over the years? How were they helpful to your celebration of the Christ Child's coming?

2. If the fabled "visitor from outer space" were to ask you to describe in simple terms what Christmas means to you, what would you say? Write one sentence on a piece of paper. Share it with others in your group.

3. How has the Christmas message changed for you over the years? At what period of your life did it seem most real? When was it absent for you?

Christmas Joy

by Stephen W. Pavey

Purpose:	To focus on Jesus as the best Christmas gift
Theme:	Busy-ness; priorities; Christmas
Scripture:	Matthew 6:19–21; Luke 2
Time:	5–7 minutes
Cast:	**Neil Overton**—age 30–40; sports commentator
	Phil Knowsall—age 30–40; sports commentator
	Lloyd Johnston—age 30–40; three-time state champion last-minute Christmas shopper; courier
	Betty Lou Fisher—age 30–40; pharmacist; has been laid up with a back injury
	Cashier—age 20–40
	Extras
Costumes:	Suits for Neil and Phil
Props:	Assorted toys, table for cashier, small manger scene set up as store decoration, basketball, 2 large bags
Lighting:	General
Sound:	Background music, bell sound, hand-held microphones for Neil and Phil
Setting:	Toy store (can be represented by tables or shelves lined with boxes and selcted toys)
Notes:	Extra actors should wander through the store, browsing and shopping as the sketch begins.

Christmas Joy

by Stephen W. Pavey

NEIL and PHIL stand downstage left, holding microphones. Fade in music.

NEIL

Good evening. I'm Neil Overton.

PHIL

And I'm Phil Knowsall.

NEIL

And welcome to another edition of Mad World of Sports, another exciting competition I'm sure you'll enjoy. We are broadcasting live from Teddy's Toy Emporium on this, another Christmas Eve, eagerly awaiting this year's competition. Phil, can you tell us who our players are?

PHIL

Sure can, Neil. As you can see, the action is already underway, as the shoppers have made their way onto the floor, ready to engage in some wild, last-minute Christmas shopping. With us tonight we have in the blue shirt, our three-time state champion, Lloyd "the packer" Johnston. Lloyd, as you may recall, Neil, is a courier by trade, and as a result, is too busy at Christmastime to do any shopping before Christmas Eve.

NEIL

I bet ya' delivering packages all year has groomed him nicely for today's competition, hasn't it, Phil?

PHIL

You bet. And squaring off against Lloyd this year is Betty Lou Fisher, a pharmacist, who as it turns out, has been laid up with a back injury until just yesterday when she was released from the hospital.

NEIL

Wow, with that kind of problem, do you think she really stands a chance against Lloyd?

PHIL

Well, I wouldn't count her out just yet, Neil. After all, on this, the last shopping day before Christmas, people can certainly surprise you. Betty Lou's in a desperate situation, so she just might surprise us.

NEIL

Well, let's watch the action as it unfolds.

LLOYD picks up an item and takes it to the CASHIER who puts it in a big bag and leaves the bag on the table. LLOYD walks past BETTY LOU and gives her a taunting smile, then continues to browse.

PHIL

Well, Neil, it looks as though Lloyd has scored first. *(BETTY LOU takes an item to the CASHIER who puts it in a bag, leaving it on the counter beside LLOYD's bag.)*

NEIL

It sure looks that way, but ... oh ... wait! Betty Lou has responded with a parcel of her own.

PHIL

I'm surprised, Neil, at the relatively slow pace we are witnessing so far, considering the store closes in mere minutes.

NEIL

Well, don't worry, Phil. I think things are about to pick up. I see Lloyd about to strike again. And it looks as though Betty Lou is right behind. *(LLOYD takes another parcel to the CASHIER following the same procedure as before, but walks faster with BETTY LOU right behind, dropping her parcel into her bag.)*

PHIL

Both players are on top of their game. What's this, Neil? I think I see trouble brewing. Both Lloyd and Betty Lou seem to be eyeing the same toy. This could mean some fierce competition. *(LLOYD and BETTY LOU, staring at the same toy across the room, each suddenly realize the other is eyeing it. They both make a mad dash toward it, leaping, with BETTY LOU acquiring the toy first.)* Ah, you see Neil, I told you not to underestimate Betty Lou.

NEIL

That you did. *(BETTY LOU races her toy to the CASHIER. She collects a few more toys and races toward the CASHIER, only to be beaten to the table by a few alert customers. LLOYD snickers at her foiled attempt.)*

PHIL

Wow, did you see that?

NEIL

Yes, I did. Looks like we have a few other competitors in the running. They performed the old squeeze play on poor Betty Lou.

BETTY LOU sneaks behind the CASHIER and bends down to speak into a microphone.

BETTY LOU

Attention shoppers: As a special in-store feature, we will be giving away free Megameltdown dolls in aisle three for the next two minutes. *(The people ahead of BETTY LOU rush offstage, leaving her to give her items to the CASHIER who puts them in her bag.)*

PHIL

(Excitedly) And it seems ol' Betty Lou squeezed them right out of the picture. She is certainly showing herself to be a real athlete here today.

NEIL

That's right, Phil. Where she might be lacking in athletics in comparison to Lloyd, she sure has him beat in the brains department.

PHIL

Looks like Lloyd is about to deliver once again. *(LLOYD picks up a basketball and starts dribbling toward BETTY LOU, who is blocking access to the CASHIER. They exchange intense stares.)* Lloyd's about to make his move. Here he goes. *(BETTY LOU reaches for the ball, but LLOYD maneuvers around her, throwing the ball, as if at a basketball hoop, into the awaiting bag, held open by the CASHIER.)* He shoots. He scores!

NEIL

He certainly does. And it would appear *(looking at his watch)* that we are almost out of time. We are in a fierce battle. These final moments will be crucial ones. And ... it appears as though Lloyd is desperately looking for something.

LLOYD

(Searching frantically, then asking CASHIER) Where're your footballs?

CASHIER

Right over here. *(She picks one off a shelf and throws it to him in front of the manger scene. BETTY LOU tries to intercept, but falls and knocks over parts of the manger scene, dropping a couple of boxes. LLOYD runs the ball to the CASHIER.)*

NEIL

Oh no, Phil. I think Betty Lou is having trouble with that back injury. *(BETTY LOU struggles to get up, but as she starts to pick up her parcel, she notices the fallen manger scene. She puts her parcels down and picks up the pieces, putting them back in place.)* That's odd. For some strange reason Betty Lou has put her parcels down and has stopped to replace the manger scene. This will almost certainly put her out of the running. Any thoughts on this bizarre move, Phil?

PHIL

The only thing I can think of is that she was afraid she would be forced to pay for any broken pieces, and would lose extra time at Customer Service. Well, it's too bad. She made some great plays.

LLOYD slowly walks over to BETTY LOU, stops briefly, then picks up her boxes.

NEIL

Wait a minute, Phil. What is Lloyd doing? Why is he picking up Betty Lou's parcels? Is this some way of rubbing defeat in her face? Well, now he's taking them over to the cashier. What? He put them in her bag! What does he think he's doing? *(A bell sounds)* And that's it. In a strange twist of fate, Betty Lou has won. The store is now closed and she has gotten her Christmas shopping done. Any idea what possessed these two competitors to just give up, Phil?

PHIL

Well, Neil, it might be because ... uh, no I don't Neil.

NEIL

Let's see if we can get a quick interview with our players. Betty Lou, Lloyd, could we have a word? *(LLOYD and BETTY LOU approach)* I want to ask you, Betty Lou, what were you thinking when you went back to the manger scene, instead of to the cashier?

BETTY LOU

Well, after I came in contact with the manger scene, I realized that I lost my focus in more ways than one. Going back to the manger scene caused me to remember that Jesus was a gift for mankind. If I'm going to celebrate that gift, I've got to get my priorities straight, and straighten up my act.

NEIL

What do you mean?

BETTY LOU

I mean, I can't let the busyness of the season cause me to focus only on myself. After all, God was thinking of us when He sent His only Son. The least I can do is show His love to others.

NEIL

And I guess it's spreading. Isn't that right Lloyd?

LLOYD

It sure is. *(Hugs NEIL)*

NEIL

Uh, that's okay, really. Until next time on the Mad World of Sports, this is Neil Overton ...

PHIL

And Phil Knowsall ...

NEIL

Saying goodnight and merry Christmas.

Actors FREEZE and EXIT.

Christmas Joy

by Stephen W. Pavey

A Note to the Pastor or Bible Study Leader:

Christmas giving, the advertising folk will explain, goes back to three Wise Men presenting gold, frankincense, and myrrh to the infant Jesus in Matthew's Gospel. More realistically, the gifts we give are a sign of our love for others in a season which celebrates God's love in Christ. It is a thin line, however, between the love feast and the greedy feeding frenzy which so often characterizes our culture's celebration of Christmas. Even committed Christians can easily cross the line.

Now, granted, it is expected that somewhere in the weeks preceding Christmas, the preacher will take some well-aimed shots at "commercial Christmas." We will scold our flocks for our blatant grasping for the Christmas goodies while Jesus lies poor and chilly in the manger. Admit it, the preacher's nagging does little good. After all, we're up against a well-organized industry which has had generations of propagandizing to mold the minds of the masses.

This year, why not use the phenomenon of gift giving (and this winsome drama) to encourage people in their stewardship? Ask your congregation or group: Why do we give of what we have to others? To God? Why max out the credit cards in toys and nonsense when our giving might become more focused on Christ and His ministry? In response to the precious, saving gift God gives to us in His Son, how about giving to homeless shelters "in the name of" a loved one, or giving to a world relief organization "in honor of" a coworker? Christmas giving could easily prove an entry point to discuss Christmas stewardship.

Questions for Study and Discussion:

1. What was the best Christmas gift you ever received? Why?

2. What was the best Christmas gift you ever gave? Why?

3. What Christmas gifts lie unused in our cellars, attics, or closets? What might we do with them?

4. Share family gift-giving customs. Are gifts given on Christmas Eve? Christmas Day? How do our customs encourage our care for one another?

5. How does John 3:16 encourage our giving? If God so loved that He gave, how might our gifts reflect His love in action?

Production Notes
Using Full-length Plays and Programs

Rehearse. Rehearse. Rehearse. Full-length plays and programs can be dynamic ministry tools but they require some work. You'll need help. Don't try to organize a full-length program by yourself. At the least, you'll need a director and a producer. The director's focus is on working with the actors during the rehearsal process to bring the script to life. The producer's job is to oversee musicians and crews working on props, costumes, set, and lighting. As with any drama, the director should have studied the script and have a vision for the performance. It is his or her job to help the actors realize that vision. It is up to the producer to help the costumer and other designers work with that vision as well. If the director tries to function as both director and producer, he or she will lose focus on the script and the performance will show it. A producer doesn't necessarily need theater experience; he or she needs to be well-organized and energetic.

In a full-length script, costumes, set, and lighting become more important. They actually help to tell the story. It may be more difficult to find professionals to help you with these areas but look for people with at least some experience. For example, a good seamstress will have experience "building" clothing. She could be helpful in costuming. An art teacher could be helpful in designing a set while a shop teacher could be in charge of building it.

As you set up your rehearsal process, don't try to rehearse the entire script at every rehearsal. Break it up into scenes or beats and rehearse only one or two of these at a time. When you've rehearsed each scene or beat several times, put the whole thing together for a rehearsal called a run-through. During the run-through, evaluate which individual scenes need more work and call additional rehearsals for those scenes. Have at least one or two full run-throughs before the actual performance. The week before the performance in a theater is called "tech week." It is during this week that all technical aspects of the show from costumes and makeup to sets and lighting come together. During this week, have at least one run-through that includes all aspects of the performance. Don't allow actors to stop during this run-through. Treat it as a performance. This allows actors to experience the entire show without a break as they will during the actual performance. It allows you to see what the entire show looks like from beginning to end without stopping. This run-through will tell you if you're ready for an audience.

If the script is to be used as part of a worship service, work with the pastor to make the entire service cohesive. If the script is a performance on its own, separate from a worship setting, make sure the audience has a message to take home with them. Keep your actors focused on what that message is and how they are helping to spread it.

A Servant's Heart

by Doug Kotwica

Purpose: To show the importance of spreading God's Word

Theme: Witnessing; Christmas

Scripture: Isaiah 7:14; Micah 5:2; Matthew 1:20–21, 28:18–20; Luke 1:30–33,

Time: 45–60 minutes

Cast: **Narrators**—can be children or adults; need 2–8 narrators total

Saint Nicholas—age 50–60; *not* Santa Claus but the real Saint Nicholas

Servant—age 8–10; a poor, young girl

Character Narrators—Moses, King David, Isaiah, Micah, Gabriel; these characters may be played by adults or children

Angels—various ages; one Angel on High plus a host of angels

Mary—mother of Jesus

Joseph—Mary's husband

Wise Men—age 30–50; need three

Animals—OPTIONAL: sheep, donkeys, camels, oxen, cattle

Costumes: Traditional biblical dress for all biblical characters; red robe for Saint Nicholas; tattered clothing for Servant; Narrators may be dressed in matching robes for consistency

Props: Doll wrapped in blankets to represent baby Jesus; manger; staffs for shepherds; gifts for Wise Men; "stone" tablets for Moses

Lighting: Spotlights or area lighting on each of the four stages

Sound: Accompaniment for traditional Christmas songs listed in the script

Setting: Action takes place on four separate stage areas. Stages 1 and 4 are bare for Narrators. Stage 3 is Saint Nicholas' church. Stage 2 represents various places from a mountain to the stable—this can be accomplished with minimal set pieces such as a manger to represent the stable.

Notes: This script is intended to use a variety of ages but it can be performed completely by children. Casting is flexible to accommodate your group size.

A Servant's Heart

by Doug Kotwica

Stage 1

NARRATOR 1

There is a time every year when the world remembers a wonderful event that happened two thousand years ago. That event was one of the greatest moments in all history, the birth of the Savior. That alone should be cause for celebration, but through the years, we have developed so many legends and traditions that we almost miss the real reason for the season. *(EXIT)*

Stage 4

NARRATOR 3

Now we have garland and Christmas trees,

Both real and pretend.

We have reindeer and tin soldiers,

And packages to send.

The latest toy to run and buy,

You shake your head and wonder, "why?"

There's apple cider and mistletoe,

A dozen parties to which you must go.

There're jingle bells and sleighs,

And all the Christmas plays.

There're cards you must send early,

And Santa's beard, white and curly.

There are rummy-tum-tums,

And little toy drums.

There are hugs and kisses and pinches,

And terrible, green, small-hearted Grinches.

There are memories from long ago,

And legends mixed with new-fallen snow.

There is so much to do to get it just right,

You might keel over before Christmas night! *(EXIT)*

Stage 1

NARRATOR 2

So tonight, we ask you to set it all aside, and join us on a journey—a journey to long ago. We are going to find out what Christmas really is. But first we need to leave our country and travel to ancient Asia Minor in the Middle East. We leave our modern day and go back in time. The year is 346. *(EXIT)*

Stage 4

NARRATOR 3

It has been a terrible year. Wars are raging on all sides, poverty and despair are everywhere. There isn't enough work, and what work there is, is hard. The rich are few and they are tight with their money. But the poor people are many and they seldom have enough food to eat or clothes to wear. It is truly a sad time. *(A light comes up on stage 3, a middle ages church; interior. As NARRATOR 3 says the following, SERVANT ENTERS.)* Tonight, a poor servant girl has found her way to a church. She has never been to a church before and doesn't know anything about God. She wanders down to the front of the church and sits down. She's the only one there and doesn't know what to expect. She just sits. After a few minutes, she hears a voice, and a man dressed in a red robe walks toward her. *(EXIT)*

Stage 3

NICHOLAS

(ENTERING) It is late to be out, my child. Can I help you?

SERVANT

Who are you?

NICHOLAS

I am the Bishop here. My name is Nicholas.

SERVANT

I have heard of you; they call you Saint Nicholas because of all the kindness you show people.

NICHOLAS

I show kindness to people because God first showed kindness toward me. Who are you?

SERVANT

I am just a poor servant. I came here to find this God you speak of. But I'm afraid He isn't interested in anyone poor and worthless like me.

NICHOLAS

Oh, that is not the case at all. Do you know what night this is?

SERVANT

No sir, I don't. Today was another working day and so is tomorrow. What is special about tonight?

NICHOLAS

Tonight is Christmas! This is the night we celebrate the birth of our Savior, Jesus. Would you like to hear about the birth of Jesus?

SERVANT

Yes sir, I would.

NICHOLAS

Then make some room for me on your chair, and I will tell you a wonderful story. Ah, it's such a beautiful night. So peaceful, so quiet. *(Sits)*

NICHOLAS and SERVANT FREEZE. Audience sings "Silent Night."

NICHOLAS

We begin at the beginning of time. After God created the world and everything in it, He created Adam and Eve. Adam and Eve were God's friends and spent their time in a garden God created for them called Eden. One day, Satan, disguised as a serpent, tempted them and they disobeyed God. God was angry and sent them out of the garden. From that moment, mankind's relationship with God changed. God still loved His people, but they often disobeyed Him. God spoke to His people through different leaders. When Moses was the leader of God's people, God gave him commandments for the people to follow. Moses met with God on a mountain.

Stage 2

MOSES

Lord God, I have come up on this mountain so that I can bring back the commandments for the people to follow. *(EXIT)*

Stage 3

NICHOLAS

Some people tried to follow God's commandments, but not one person could follow them without any mistakes. God promised to send a Savior to save the people from their sins. He told King David hundreds of years before it would happen that He was going to do this, so David began telling everyone that God was going to save them.

Stage 2

KING DAVID

"Show me Your ways O LORD, teach me Your paths; guide me in Your truth and teach me, for You are God, my Savior, and my hope is in You all the day long" (Psalm 25:4–5). *(EXIT)*

NICHOLAS

Once the people knew that a Savior was coming, God used prophets like Isaiah and Micah to explain the details of His plan. This was seven hundred years before the birth of Jesus.

SERVANT

That is amazing.

Stage 2

ISAIAH

"Therefore the Lord Himself will give you a sign: The virgin will be with child and will give birth to a Son, and will call Him Immanuel" (Isaiah 7:14). *(EXIT)*

MICAH

"But you, Bethlehem Ephrathah, though you are small among the clans of Judah, out of you will come for me one who will be ruler over Israel, whose origins are from of old, from ancient times" (Micah 5:2). *(EXIT)*

NICHOLAS and SERVANT FREEZE. Audience sings "O Little Town of Bethlehem."

NICHOLAS

Once the prophets had told the people that a Savior was coming, they began looking for Him and studying the time of His coming. But then ... the prophets said nothing. For 400 years God was silent. The people waited and waited. And they sang to God to bring the Savior, who would be called Emmanuel, which means God with us.

NICHOLAS and SERVANT FREEZE. Audience sings "O Come, O Come, Emmanuel."

NICHOLAS

And then it was time. God chose a hard-working carpenter named Joseph and his future wife Mary. *(MARY and JOSEPH ENTER on Stage 2—The scene is their home).* They were to be the parents of the Savior. They had committed their lives to God and would do whatever He asked them to do. How could they ever have imagined what a wonderful job God would give them? They would raise and protect the Savior of the entire world. Mary would be Jesus' mother, and Joseph would be Jesus' stepfather. And so it was that the Holy Spirit came upon Mary and she became pregnant.

SERVANT

Did Joseph know what was happening?

NICHOLAS

At first, neither of them knew what was happening. Then the angel Gabriel came to Mary and explained. But she was scared, so Gabriel told her ...

GABRIEL

(Stage 2 with MARY, JOSEPH aside) "Do not be afraid, Mary, you have found favor with God. You will be with child and give birth to a son, and you are to give Him the name Jesus. He will be great and will be called the Son of the Most High. The Lord God will give Him the throne of His father David, and He will reign over the house of Jacob forever; His kingdom will never end" (Luke 1:30–33).

NICHOLAS

It became obvious that Mary was pregnant, and Joseph knew that he wasn't the father, so he decided that he would have to leave Mary quietly. God didn't want Joseph to leave, so He had an angel appear to him in a dream. And the angel said ...

GABRIEL

(Stage 2 with JOSPEH, MARY aside) "Joseph son of David, do not be afraid to take Mary home as your wife, because what is conceived in her is from the Holy Spirit. She will give birth to a son, and you are to give Him the name Jesus, because He will save His people from their sins" (Matthew 1:20–21). *(GABRIEL, MARY, and JOSEPH EXIT)*

NICHOLAS

And when Joseph woke up, he did all that the angel had told him. And then it was time ...

Stage 4

NARRATOR 4

"In those days Caesar Augustus issued a decree that a census should be taken of the entire Roman world. ... And everyone went to his own town to register. So Joseph also went up from the town of Nazareth in Galilee to Judea, to Bethlehem the town of David, because he belonged to the house and line of David. He went there to register with Mary, who was pledged to be married to him and was expecting a child. While they were there, the time came for the baby to be born ... (Luke 2:1–6). *(EXIT)*

JOSEPH and MARY ENTER Stage 2. The scene is the stable.

NICHOLAS

Since there were hundreds of people in Bethlehem to be counted for the census, all the rooms at the inns were taken. Joseph and Mary searched long and hard for a place to sleep, but with no success. Since the baby was to be born any time, they had to find some place, any place! An innkeeper offered them his stable, where they would at least be out of the weather. And there the child was born, and Mary laid Him in a manger—a feeding bin.

NICHOLAS and SERVANT FREEZE. Audience sings "Away in a Manger."

NICHOLAS

Angels went out to announce to the world that the Savior had been born. The first to find out were not the kings and leaders, but the lowly shepherds.

SHEPHERDS ENTER stage 1. The scene is nighttime in the hills. NARRATOR ENTERS stage 4.

NARRATOR 5

"And there were shepherds living out in the fields nearby, keeping watch over their flocks at night. An angel of the Lord appeared to them, and the glory of the Lord shown around them, and they were terrified. But the angel said to them ... (Luke 2:8–10) *(EXIT)*

ANGEL ON HIGH

"Do not be afraid. I bring you good news of great joy that will be for all the people. Today in the town of David a Savior has been born to you; He is Christ the Lord" (Luke 2:10–11). *(EXIT)*

ALL ACTORS except ANGELS FREEZE. Audience sings "Angels We Have Heard on High." ANGELS sing along.

NARRATOR 6

(ENTERING stage 4) And then the angel said to them, "This will be a sign to you: you will find a baby wrapped in cloths and lying in a manger" (Luke 2:12).

MORE ANGELS ENTER stage 1 with SHEPHERDS.

NARRATOR 6

"Suddenly a great company of the heavenly host appeared with the angel, praising God and saying, 'Glory to God in the highest, and on earth peace to men on whom His favor rests.' "(Luke 2:13–14). *(EXIT)*

ACTORS FREEZE. Audience sings "Hark, the Herald Angels Sing." ANGELS EXIT after this song.

NARRATOR 7

(ENTERS stage 4) "When the angels had left them and gone into heaven, the shepherds said to one another, 'Let's go to Bethlehem, and see this thing that has happened, which the Lord told us about' " (Luke 2:15). *(EXIT)*

SHEPHERDS cross to stage 3 as the audience sings "O Come All Ye Faithful."

NARRATOR 8

(ENTERS stage 4) "So they hurried off and found Mary and Joseph, and the baby, who was lying in the manger. When they had seen Him, they spread the word concerning what had been told to them about this child, and all who heard it were amazed at what the shepherds said to them" (Luke 2:16–18). *(EXIT)*

Audience sings "Go Tell It on the Mountain."

NICHOLAS

Eventually news of His birth went far and wide. A group of Wise Men from the East had been studying God's Word and waiting for the Savior. They had added up the years from Old Testament prophecies and knew that the Savior, Jesus, had been born. They began a long journey to find Him. As they traveled westward, they followed a star, a wonderful star that always seemed to guide them.

3 WISE MEN ENTER stage 1. It is night. Audience sings "We Three Kings." WISE MEN cross to stage 2 to join MARY and JOSEPH. The manger is gone. Stage 2 is bare.

NICHOLAS

When the Wise Men found Jesus and His family, they found Him in Nazareth and brought Him gifts fit for a king—gold, frankincense, and myrrh. And they pledged their lives and hearts to this boy king.

ACTORS FREEZE while audience sings "O Holy Night."

SERVANT

So even the wisest kings on earth bowed down to Jesus.

NICHOLAS

They were wise enough to know who He was and humble enough to accept Him as their Lord.

SERVANT

So He came to save the shepherds and the kings, the lowest *and* the highest.

NICHOLAS

That was the reason for the birth of the Savior. He was born into this world to live as a man, and to live the perfect life. Then He stood in our place and accepted the punishment for our sins. He could do that because He was God and loved us enough to give Himself in our place as payment for our sins. Our only requirement is to believe in Him. And we can live with Him in heaven forever.

SERVANT

Even a lowly servant like me can go to heaven?

NICHOLAS

Yes. Do you believe that Jesus is God and that He died and rose again to pay the price for your sins?

SERVANT

I do believe in Jesus as my Savior.

NICHOLAS

The angels are rejoicing in heaven!

SERVANT

I have heard such stories of your kindness and about the gifts you give to the children, but you have given me the greatest gift of all.

Audience and ACTORS sing "Joy to the World."

A Servant's Heart

by Doug Kotwica

A Note to the Pastor or Bible Study Leader:

Telling the good news of God's salvation in Jesus Christ is so natural at Christmas. It is difficult not to get the point that in Jesus Christ, our Immanuel, God is coming very near to us. The carols we hear in the shopping malls and on the radio proclaim it. The cards sent by friends into our homes depict it. Church on Christmas Eve or Day seems just, well, natural.

Yet the "natural" part of Christmas evangelism can also be its downfall. When a message is so familiar, it can also become trite. How sad that the world can hear the Christmas Gospel and put it into the compartment of "tradition" rather than life-altering reality. Jesus is forced to share the spotlight with Santa, the Grinch, and Frosty—and guess who often is upstaged!

For that reason, Christians turn to the rich treasures of tradition to bring the Christmas message home in different ways. Our drama places Bishop Nicholas of Myra as the speaker of the evangel. He was hardly a "jolly old elfe," this 4th century church father, but his legendary compassion and love for Jesus and others puts him in the perfect position to announce the Christmas Gospel as forcefully as he lived it out. A commentary on Nicholas is found in *Festivals and Commemorations* by Phillip Pfatteicher, pages 442–443 (Augsburg Publishing, Minneapolis, 1980).

Questions for Study and Discussion:

1. How does your congregation allow the Christmas clebration to be an opportunity for evangelism? How might you use evangelism more effectively at Christmas time?

2. Who preached the Gospel most effectively to you at Christmas? A child? A teacher or pastor? A friend or parent?

3. How might Santa Claus be "re-sanctified" as St. Nicholas in your congregation? Might a visit from St. Nicholas or Santa, proclaiming the Gospel of God's love, be an appropriate part of your Christmas celebration?

A Christmas Peace

by Tim Wesemann

Purpose: To make Christ's peace a conversation piece

Theme: Peace; Christmas

Scripture: Luke 2; Matthew 2

Time: 60 minutes

Cast: **Speakers**—adults or older children

Children—grades kindergarten through eighth grade, any number of children

Costumes: Biblical costumes for children portraying Mary, Joseph, Shepherds, and Angels in the retelling of the Christmas story.

Props: Manger; doll to represent baby Jesus; gifts to hand out to the congregation

Lighting: General

Sound: Accompaniment for songs listed in the script

Setting: Various

Notes: In the middle of the presentation, children will move into the congregation to distribute gifts such as Christmas cassettes, videos, Bibles, books, pictures of manger scenes drawn by the children, and essays about the true meaning of Christmas. Be creative. Ask children to donate items or make it a class project to draw pictures or write essays to distribute. The congregation will be told that these gifts are to be used to help them continue conversing about Christ's peace.

A Christmas Peace

by Tim Wesemann

The congregation sings "Oh Come All Ye Faithful." The children process in from the back of the church. Two heralding trumpets make an archway at the front of the church. Banners may hang from them as though announcing Christ's birth.

PASTOR

In the name of the Father ...

PEOPLE

Who created us and loved us enough to send His only Son to die in our place so that we can have the gift of peace through the forgiveness of sins and eternal life.

PASTOR

In the name of the Son, Jesus Christ, whose birth we celebrate this evening.

PEOPLE

He is the Prince of Peace for a hostile world. He has spoken to us through His Word along with His life-giving death on the cross and His resurrection on Easter morning.

PASTOR

In the name of the Holy Spirit ...

PEOPLE

Who brought heaven to us through the gift of faith, which will be strengthened tonight as we hear God's life-giving Word.

PASTOR

In the name of the Father and of the Son and of the Holy Spirit.

PEOPLE

Amen!

PASTOR

Let us join our hearts in prayer. It is a holy night, Father of Love, and we are on holy ground in Your presence. Bring Bethlehem near tonight while leading us near Bethlehem's glory. Cause us to marvel and stand in awe. Lead us to worship the newborn King.

PEOPLE

Let us hear Your voice speaking personally and clearly to us through the voices and actions of Your children. May our faith be strengthened and Your peace be realized in our lives.

PASTOR

Bless not only the message shared here tonight but also the same life-giving message of our Savior's birth which is being shared this week all around the world. Bless the missionaries bringing Your story for the first time. Bless the holy conversations of Jesus' birth spoken on telephones, communicated in cards and letters, through home devotions and radio programs, and through services lead by pastors, laypeople, and school children.

PEOPLE

Unleash the full power of the Holy Spirit that lives may be changed through the peace that Jesus brings through His life. In Jesus' holy name we worship, pray, and live. Amen.

Congregation sings "O Little Town of Bethlehem." As congregation sings, the KINDERGARTNERS, FIRST, and SECOND GRADERS ENTER the chancel. CHILDREN may be lined up across the front of the chancel or placed in different parts of the church.

SPEAKER 1

Tonight's service has as its theme, "Christ's Birth—A Conversation Peace." If you noticed the spelling of the word *peace*, you noted the play on words. But it's more than that. We pray that the words shared tonight will make a difference in your life. And more than the words, the Word who became flesh and dwells among us. His name is Jesus and He has come to bring you peace.

SPEAKER 2

You may have conversation pieces, spelled p-i-e-c-e-s, in your home or work place. They are items people may notice and start talking about. They may be pieces that tell their own interesting story.

SPEAKER 3

Jesus is a conversation *peace*. His is a telling story. His is a story of peace that He brings you tonight in order to change all your tomorrows. We love to tell His story and we are thankful for all who have shared His story with us. Listen now, as His story unfolds.

KINDERGARTNERS, FIRST, and SECOND GRADERS take their places to share the following:

CHILD 1

The story of the birth of Jesus is a telling one.

CHILD 2

It started with a conversation between God and Adam and Eve.

CHILD 3

God came one day to talk with Adam and Eve. They were trying to hide from Him because they had sinned.

CHILD 4

But God knew where they were because He knows all things.

CHILD 5

In their conversation, God told Adam and Eve that Someone would come to save them from their sins.

CHILD 6

So God told Adam and Eve about the Savior.

CHILD 7

Adam and Eve shared the story with their children and their grandchildren.

CHILD 8

Down through the years, people looked forward to the One who would save them.

CHILD 9

The prophets told the people about the Savior who would come. The people told their family and friends.

CHILD 10

The angel Gabriel told Mary. An angel also told Joseph about Jesus' birth.

CHILD 11

Mary told Elizabeth, her relative. Elizabeth told Zechariah.

CHILD 12

Joseph told the story to the innkeepers.

CHILD 13

Angels told the shepherds through song. The shepherds told everyone they met.

CHILD 14

Later on, the star told the Wise Men. The Wise Men told Herod.

CHILD 15

I think the Wise Men told the easterners, when they arrived home.

KINDERGARTEN CLASS

We know the story of Jesus' birth
How from heaven He came to earth.
This story we find in God's holy book
With parents and teachers we take a look.
The Bible tells us that Christ is the Way—

He's the way to heaven, where one day we'll stay.
Let's travel to Bethlehem and worship our kin
The Way—in a manger! Come now, let's sing.

Children sing "Away in a Manger."

CHILD 16

The story of Jesus and His birth is more than just another story.

KINDERGARTNERS, FIRST, AND SECOND GRADERS

Jesus is the Prince of Peace.

CHILD 17

And we all need to know that peace can be ours because the world is filled with:

CHILD 18

Hurtfulness and hatefulness; war and wickedness; hunger and hopelessness; problems and pressures;

CHILD 19

But tonight we are talking about peace.

KINDERGARTNERS, FIRST, AND SECOND GRADERS

Jesus is the Prince of Peace.

CHILD 20

Jesus brings us peace through the forgiveness of sins and eternal life.

CHILD 21

What a truth to believe in, what a joy to know, what a privilege to tell!

KINDERGARTNERS, FIRST, AND SECOND GRADERS

Jesus is the Prince of Peace!

CHILD 22

He is *our* peace. He is *our* Lord! Christ the Child is Lord of all!

Children sing "Infant Holy, Infant Lowly."

Congregation sings "It Came Upon a Midnight Clear." As the congregation sings, KINDERGARTNERS, FIRST, and SECOND GRADERS return to their seats and THIRD, FOURTH, and FIFTH GRADERS come forward into the chancel to tell who shared the story of Jesus and His peace with them.

CHILD 1

The story of Jesus' birth certainly is a telling one. It is also an amazing story.

CHILD 2

Jesus was a child who was born to die—so that we could live.

CHILD 3

We have relatives, friends, and teachers who love us so much that they took the time to tell us about Jesus' birth, life, death, and resurrection.

CHILD 4

We have learned that there is no one who loves us more than Jesus.

CHILD 5

He loved us so much that He gave His life for us, in our place.

CHILD 6

His story of love for me is an awesome one. I'm amazed and astonished at why Jesus would love me that much. But I believe He does. And just in case you were wondering, He loves you that much too.

CHILDREN sing "I Wonder as I Wander."

THIRD, FOURTH, AND FIFTH GRADERS

We have learned about Jesus and His birth from many different people and in many different ways. We are thankful for those people who have taught us. We love to celebrate Jesus' birth and life. Listen now to some of the ways we have learned about Jesus' birth.

The following section should be written by the children, sharing how they first heard the story of Jesus' birth. Pick a variety of ways the message of Jesus was communicated with them—through parents, Sunday school teachers, vacation Bible school, books, videos, etc. A grouping of 6–12 personal examples should be used. The following are samples from the original production.

CHILD 1

I first learned that Christmas was about Christ from my parents and grandma, when I was very little. But the first time I really understood was when I started school. Now I try to explain it to my sister in simple words because she in only 4. I also have a sister born on Christmas! When we get older I'll tell her about the blessing she has of having the same birthday as Christ.

CHILD 2

I first learned that Christmas is about Jesus in Sunday school. I was 3. I heard a story called, "The Birth of Jesus." My family celebrates Christ's birthday by reading about His birth.

CHILD 3

I was about 3 years old when I learned about Christmas. My mom and dad and big brother told me that we celebrated Jesus' birthday. I thought that was pretty neat. When Christmas came, I made a Christmas card that said, "Happy Birthday, Jesus!" and I asked my mom to send it to Jesus.

CHILD 4

I first learned that Christmas is about Jesus when my mom read me a Christmas book about Jesus. My family celebrates Christ's birthday by listening to Christmas songs.

CHILD 5

I first learned that Christmas is about Christ when I was 8 months old because my family reads the story of Jesus' birth every year. We also have a calendar to count down the days until Christmas.

CHILD 6

I first learned that Christmas is about Christ when my family and I went to my cousin's house and my aunt told me about Him. I like to celebrate Christmas by going to my grandma's and grandpa's house.

CHILD 7

The first time I heard the Christmas story was from my preschool teacher. I was sitting by her with the other kids, singing songs. Then she told us to sit in a circle around the tree. She told us what Christmas was all about. When she was done we all began to make noises of astonishment!

CHILD 8

The first time I heard the Christmas story, my grandma told it to me when I was 5. She sat on the rocking chair, and I sat on her lap. She told me that Christmas was not just about presents. Then she read the Christmas story to me from a book.

CHILD 9

One of the first people to share the Christmas story with me was my kindergarten teacher. When she explained it to me, it was most likely with a little storybook. The first time I heard the story it didn't mean much to me, but now it means a lot. If I could meet my kindergarten teacher again I would thank her for telling me the story of Christmas.

CHILD 10

The first person who told me the Christmas story was my grandpa. He got out his Bible and told me about Jesus' birth. When I heard it I was sitting on his lap in the family room.

CHILD 11

Every year we prepare for Christmas by lighting the Advent wreath. Each night we light the candles and one of us picks a Christmas hymn to sing. Whenever it is my youngest brother's turn, he picks, "Rudolph the Red-Nosed Reindeer." We sing it to keep him happy! Then we blow out the candles.

CHILD 12

I remember when I was about 3 or 4 and some kids from church did a play. I was chosen to be Mary. But I called myself "Murry." My doll was baby Jesus. I was really excited and I sang very loudly. That's the first time I remember being told of the birth of Jesus. Every year my family goes to the Christmas Eve service. Then we go in our living room, turn out the lights, and read the story of Jesus' birth.

CHILD 13

The first people who shared the Christmas story with me were my mom and dad. We have a calendar with pictures of the nativity scene. The first time I remember hearing the Christmas story was when I was 3. My mom said, "Christmas isn't just about Santa; it is Jesus' birthday. God loves you so much that He sent His Son, Jesus, for you and me!"

CHILD 14

I found out the true meaning of Christmas when my brother was baby Jesus in a Christmas play. Since he was in it, I focused on it more and I found out the true meaning of Christmas.

CHILD 1

As you have heard, we have learned about the birth of Jesus in many ways and from many people.

CHILD 2

We also want to tell others about Jesus, who is our conversation peace!

CHILD 3

We have learned about Jesus from the Bible, family members, teachers, pastors, and friends. We also have learned His story of peace from books, songs, videos, pictures, nativity scenes, and many other ways. Tonight we are sharing His story with you.

CHILD 4

We would also like to give some of you the gift of Jesus in a special way. Please accept the conversation pieces we bring to you while you sing "Hark, the

Herald Angels Sing." You may want to use the gifts to share Jesus' saving story with others.

Congregation sings "Hark, the Herald Angels Sing." As they sing, the THIRD, FOURTH, and FIFTH GRADERS move among the congregation handing out Christmas cassettes, videos, Bibles, books, pictures of manger scenes drawn by the children, and essays about the true meaning of Christmas, so the idea of conversing about "The Peace" will continue. As this happens, the SIXTH, SEVENTH, and EIGHTH GRADERS come forward into the chancel.

STUDENTS will act out the story of Jesus' birth as it is narrated.

CHILD 1

We've been sharing with you the fact that Jesus' birth is a telling story of peace. We've told you how we learned Jesus' salvation story. But we also want to tell you the story of Jesus' birth. It is recorded in the second chapter of Luke and the second chapter of Matthew.

STUDENTS dressed as the biblical characters ENTER through the center aisle at appropriate times as the following story unfolds. They take their places in the chancel area.

CHILD 2

"And it came to pass in those days, that there went out a decree from Caesar Augustus, that all the world should be taxed. (And this taxing was first made when Cyrenius was governor of Syria.) And all went to be taxed, every one into his own city.

CHILD 3

And Joseph also went up from Galilee, out of the city of Nazareth, into Judea, unto the city of David, which is called Bethlehem; (because he was of the house and lineage of David:) To be taxed with Mary his espoused wife, being great with child.

CHILD 4

And so it was, that, while they were there, the days were accomplished that she should be delivered. And she brought forth her first-born son, and wrapped Him in swaddling clothes, and laid Him in a manger; because there was no room for them in the inn.

CHILD 5

And there were in the same country shepherds abiding in the field, keeping watch over their flock by night. And, lo, the angel of the Lord came upon them, and the glory of the Lord shone round about them: and they were sore afraid. And the angel said unto them,

CHILD 6

Fear not: for, behold, I bring you good tidings of great joy, which shall be to all people. For unto you is born this day in the city of David a Savior, which is Christ the Lord. And this shall be a sign unto you; Ye shall find the babe wrapped in swaddling clothes, lying in a manger.

CHILD 7

And suddenly there was with the angel a multitude of the heavenly host praising God, and saying,

ALL CHILDREN

Glory to God in the highest, and on earth peace, good will toward men.

CHILD 8

And it came to pass, as the angels were gone away from them into heaven, the shepherds said one to another, Let us now go even unto Bethlehem, and see this thing which is come to pass, which the Lord has made known unto us.

CHILD 9

And they came with haste, and found Mary, and Joseph, and the babe lying in a manger. And when they had seen it, they made known abroad the saying which was told them concerning this child. And all they that heard it wondered at those things which were told them by the shepherds. But Mary kept all these things, and pondered them in her heart" (Luke 2:1–19 KJV).

CHILD 10

Now sometime after Jesus' birth, Wise Men came from the east to Jerusalem saying: "Where is He that is born King of the Jews? For we have seen His star in the east and have come to worship Him.

Child 11

When Herod the king heard these things, he was troubled, and all Jerusalem with him. ... And he sent them to Bethlehem, and said, Go and search diligently for the young child; and when ye have found Him, bring me word again, that I may come and worship Him also. When they had heard the king, they departed; and, lo, the star, which they saw in the east, went before them, till it came and stood over where the young child was. When they saw the star, they rejoiced with exceeding great joy.

Child 12

And when they were come into the house, they saw the young child with Mary his mother, and fell down, and worshiped Him: and when they had opened their treasures, they presented unto Him gifts; gold, and frankincense, and myrrh. And being warned of God in a dream that they should not return to Herod, they departed into their own country another way" (Matthew 2:1–12 KJV).

Child 13

The first people who heard the story of Jesus—a conversation peace—were in awe of God's presence with them. They glorified and praised God. They pondered the wonder of it all.

Child 14

Immanuel, God is with us. Should we not also gasp and sing, sigh and shout, see the thrill of it all, while praying and praising our gracious God? Indeed we should, because Peace came to earth on the chosen night in Bethlehem, just as it has tonight for us.

CHILDREN sing "Peace Came to Earth."

Speaker 1

Bethlehem and its most holy Child, Jesus, were brought near to us tonight. We pray you felt the peace, experienced the awe, and worshiped Him in spirit and truth.

Speaker 2

We also pray that, like the Wise Men, you will go home tonight by a different route. We pray your life was changed by the conversations we have had about our Savior, Jesus Christ. His is a telling story that needs to be told so all the world might know of His daily and eternal peace.

SPEAKER 3

We don't want to rush from the manger yet we need to continue on, telling everyone what we have learned about our Savior. Along the way, we want to thank God for all the people He has sent to touch our lives with the peace of Christ. That is the type of Christmas we want this year and every year—a Christmas focused on Jesus and His birth, which is truly a conversation peace in the center of our lives.

CHILDREN sing "Son of God, Which Christmas Is It?"

SPEAKER 1

The conversation peace was created in the heart of God. The conversation started with a voice that came down to earth from heaven. It was the voice of God speaking words of hope and peace to a sinful world.

SPEAKER 2

God continues to converse with us today through His Word and Sacraments. The gift of peace and the sharing of Christ's peace is ours to thank God for every day.

SPEAKER 3

God's conversation peace is for all of us who live in a time of upheaval, unrest, shame, and rebellion.

SPEAKER 1

The conversation peace, spelled, p-e-a-c-e, is Jesus Christ. He has come to save you and me from our sins. It's a story that is life-changing. It's a story that needs to be told. Make Jesus Christ your daily conversation peace.

SPEAKER 2

God's peace be with you, in the form of Jesus, the child born to die—the One who came to live within you and your world.

SPEAKER 3

Jesus—You are our conversation peace this Christmas and throughout the year!

CHILDREN sing "Jesus, My Conversation Peace."

The congregation sings "Silent Night."

Jesus, My Conversation Peace

Tim Wesemann

John Wittmayer

1 Je - sus, my con - ver - sa - tion peace Your
2 Je - sus, my con - ver - sa - tion peace, Born
3 Je - sus, my con - ver - sa - tion peace, We,
4 Je - sus, my con - ver - sa - tion peace, I

sto - ry's ver - y tell - ing.
in a low - ly man - ger.
like the great old shep - herds,
want the world to know

It tells of love from heav'n a - bove, Of
The Prince of Peace is now Your name, Sal -
Have stopped to wor - ship, then We'll tell The
That You have peace and joy for them. Let's

peace that has no end - ing.
va - tion is Your sto - ry.
good news to all oth - ers.
tell the world Your sto - ry.

A Christmas Peace

by Tim Wesemann

A Note to the Pastor or Bible Study Leader:

At one time in the United States it was popular to greet one another with two fingers raised in a "V" sign and a mumbled "peace." That 60s greeting has gone out of fashion in our culture, but it still is a very proper greeting in the Middle East. "Shalom," they will say in Israel. "Salaam mah," in Arab countries. The meaning is the same: "Peace."

Peace is more than the absence of conflict. It is the wholeness of life which God had originally inteded for humanity. When all things are working together—one's relationship to God and others, the environment, and oneself—then there is truly "peace." The reality of sin is the antithesis of peace, for sin breaks us apart. It tears down those precious relationships. The serpent in Eden's garden gives a deadly pitch to the woman: "Did God really say, 'You must not eat ...'?" (Genesis 3:1). With that relationship called into question, the harmonious peace which the first family had known is no longer.

The Christmas peace which the children proclaim in this drama is God's bringing all things together through a Child born in a stable long ago. Jesus is God's "shalom" made flesh. The great fissures of sin which mar and weaken our humanity are sealed by Jesus' death on the cross. They are declared invalid by God in an Easter victory that we will share on our last day. "Peace" begins this Christmas with God's sending of His Son. All things come together in Him, our peace that passes all understanding!

Questions for Study and Discussion:

1. How has a child witnessed to you of God's love?

2. Bishop D. T. Niles once said that evangelism is "one beggar telling another beggar where he has found bread." Discuss. How is that a helpful definition? What might you add?

3. How do you respond to the image of Jesus as a "conversation peace"? In your home, how do you talk about Jesus? If you don't talk about Him, why not?

4. How might you, in your daily calling, make Jesus your "conversation peace"?

Song Index

Following is a list of songs referred to in *A Servant's Heart* (*SH* below) and *A Christmas Peace* (*CP* below) and hymnals or songbooks in which the songs can be found. If you cannot find a particular song, feel free to substitute.

"Angels We Have Heard on High" *(SH):* Traditional. *Lutheran Worship* (St. Louis, Missouri: Concordia Publishing House, 1982), hymn 55.

"Away in a Manger" *(SH, CP):* Traditional. *Lutheran Worship* (St. Louis, Missouri: Concordia Publishing House, 1982), hymn 64.

"Go Tell It on the Mountain" *(SH):* Traditional. *Lutheran Worship* (St. Louis, Missouri: Concordia Publishing House, 1982), hymn 504.

"Hark, the Herald Angels Sing" *(SH, CP):* Traditional. *Lutheran Worship* (St. Louis, Missouri: Concordia Publishing House, 1982), hymn 49.

"I Wonder as I Wander" *(CP): With One Voice* (Minneapolis, Minnesota: Augsburg Fortress, 1995) #642

"Infant Holy, Infant Lowly" *(CP): Hymnal Supplement 98* (St. Louis, Missouri: Concordia Publishing House, 1998), hymn 812.

"It Came Upon a Midnight Clear" *(CP):* Traditional. *Lutheran Worship* (St. Louis, Missouri: Concordia Publishing House, 1982), hymn 62.

"Joy to the World" *(SH):* Traditional. *Lutheran Worship* (St. Louis, Missouri: Concordia Publishing House, 1982), hymn 53.

"O Holy Night" *(SH):* Traditional. *Christmas in Song* (Chicago, Illinois: Rubank Inc., 1947). (See also Hal Leonard Corp., Milwaukee, Wisconsin.)

"O Little Town of Bethlehem" *(SH, CP):* Traditional. *Lutheran Worship* (St. Louis, Missouri: Concordia Publishing House, 1982), hymn 59, 60.

"Oh Come, Oh Come, Emmanuel" *(SH):* Traditional. *Lutheran Worship* (St. Louis, Missouri: Concordia Publishing House, 1982), hymn 31.

"Oh, Come, All Ye Faithful" *(SH, CP):* Traditional. *Lutheran Worship* (St. Louis, Missouri: Concordia Publishing House, 1982), hymn 41.

"Peace Came to Earth" *(CP): With One Voice* (Minneapolis, Minnesota: Augsburg Fortress, 1995) #641

"Silent Night" *(SH, CP):* Traditional. *Lutheran Worship* (St. Louis, Missouri: Concordia Publishing House, 1982), hymn 68.

"Son of God, Which Christmas Is It?" *(CP): See This Wonder* (St. Louis, Missouri: Concordia Publishing House, 1994) #716

"We Three Kings" *(SH):* Traditional (also called "Kings of Orient"). *The Oxford Book of Carols* (London, England: Oxford University Press, 1928, 1961) page 195.

Scripts

InterMission Scripts are a dynamic way to get people to sit up and take notice in your services. They're short (five to ten minutes long) and use natural dialogue, easy staging, and a limited number of performers. The information you need—time, cast, costumes, props, sound, lighting, and setting—is on the first page for quick reference. Each Christ-centered script includes a clearly stated purpose, theme, Scripture reference, and discussion questions.

REPRODUCiBLE

unlimited, **ROYALTY-FREE** use!

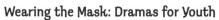

Wearing the Mask: Dramas for Youth
Deals with real-life issues: peer pressure, dating, being responsible, witnessing, more. *13 scripts*
ISBN 0-570-05376-5   12-3427 $14.99

Strong and Sturdy: Dramas for Children
One full-length play based on the book of Esther, plus three others, 3–7 minutes long. *4 scripts*
ISBN 0-570-05389-7   12-4016 $12.99

Fearless Pharoah FooFoo and Other Dramas for Children
Dramas for 6- to 12-year-olds. Minimal preparation; maximum enjoyment. *34 dramas*
ISBN 0-570-05332-3   12-3380 $14.99

Command Performances: Playing with the Ten Commandments
11 simple scripts make learning the Ten Commandments child's play for children ages 6–12.
ISBN 0-570-05370-6   12-3421 $12.99

Anticipation: Dramas for Advent
Discover the significance of time spent awaiting the birth of Christ through these living reflections on the meaning of God's arrival among His people. *14 scripts*
ISBN 0-570-05386-2   12-4014 $12.99

Celebration: Dramas for Christmas
Reflect on the meaning of Christ's birth to you personally—and the role you play each day as a follower of Christ—with these thoughtful, funny, joy-filled Christmas dramas. *7 scripts*
ISBN 0-570-05387-0   12-4015 $12.99

Preparation: Dramas for Lent
Gain a more personal understanding of the utter helplessness and fear early Christians experienced as they watched Christ crucified—until the moment they knew He had risen for them. *8 scripts*
ISBN 0-570-05391-9   12-4018 $12.99

Jubilation: Dramas for Easter
Cut through the clutter and distractions of daily life. Use these dramas to turn a spotlight on the single event that makes every moment of every day a cause for hope and joy. *7 scripts*
ISBN 0-570-05390-0   12-4017 $12.99

CPH.
Concordia Publishing House